Positive Discipline

The Complete Guide to Nurturing Your Child through Self Discipline and Problem Solving

Written By

Daniel Faber

been executed to present accurate, up to date, reliable, complete information. No warranties of any kind are declared or implied. Readers acknowledge that the author is not engaging in the rendering of legal, financial, medical or professional advice. The content within this book has been derived from various sources. Please consult a licensed professional before attempting any techniques outlined in this book.

By reading this document, the reader agrees that under no circumstances is the author responsible for any losses, direct or indirect, that are incurred as a result of the use of information contained within this document, including, but not limited to, errors, omissions, or inaccuracies.

Daniel Faber

Table of Contents

INTRODUCTION

I will start the introduction by saying that it is my true belief that each parent-child relationship is sacred, and nobody should tell a mother or a father what is best for their baby. The simple idea of giving instructions on how to educate their children always felt wrong to me.

However, I discovered that so many parents look for guidance and want to become better when educating their kids. The number is so impressive; therefore, it cannot be ignored and it gave me the idea of writing this *"how-to"* book.

After doing some research, I realized that there are plenty of books talking about the topic of positive discipline on the market, so I gave up on the idea for a long time.

The desire to start this project came back to me after one of my friends, who recently became a mother, told me that she bought a book on positive discipline but she understood nothing from it. She was complaining that the book had hard-to-understand words and it lacked examples.

After I explained to her the book's notions and what the author wanted to say, she encouraged me to start writing but to do it in such a way that even the most uneducated parents will understand how to apply the techniques of correct positive discipline.

So, here I am trying to give you an introduction to my work. I don't want to say more about the topic because there is plenty of time for that. You have a full book in front of you talking about what to do and what not to do if you want to give proper, positive discipline to your child.

Instead, I want to ask you to overcome the temptation of skipping some chapters and read only the parts that you think you are interested in. You might find valuable information where you least expect. Also, keep a notebook around and write down everything you find meaningful in such a way to create a personal record for you to check from time to time.

Lastly, read the book slowly. If the methods you read in this book make sense to you, you might want to make some changes, and it is easier to change a little at a time than all at once. After you've read a chapter, lay the book aside and give yourself time to digest the information before moving on to the next one.

So, this is it! I hope that you will enjoy the book and find the facts stated in it helpful. Let's begin!

CHAPTER ONE

POSITIVE DISCIPLINE - INTRODUCTORY NOTIONS

Before going into more depth on the subject of how to discipline a child, I think that it is mandatory to really understand the notion of *"Positive Discipline"*, which is, after all, the main title of this book.

So, positive discipline, also known as PD, is a model for correcting children with the purpose of teaching them what is good and what is bad. Simply put, it is the approach to teach them how to behave and how to be disciplined.

This model is used in schools but is also recommended to be applied by parents, and it concentrates on the positive parts of the child's behavior.

The method belongs to Dr. Jane Nelsen, and it is based on the ideas presented by Rudolf Dreikurs and Alfred Adler. Even if you are not the biggest history fan, I still think that you should know a thing or two about the role the two doctors had in the development of what is now called positive discipline. Because of this, I ask you to bear with me for a few minutes and continue reading.

What is Positive Discipline - Its History and Development

It all started when, in the 1920s, Dr. Alfred Adler presented a new notion to the public of the United States of America. He stood there and talked about a subject nobody ever touched before - parenting education.

He spoke about how children need to be treated with respect by their parents and supervisors without being spoiled or pampered. He advanced a theory that stated that a child raised in this manner would have fewer chances to grow up with behavioral and therefore social issues.

Around the same years, some classroom techniques on the subjects were presented in Vienna, but it took more than a decade for them to be displayed for the US public, and the one who made it possible was Dr. Dreikurs.

The part that I want you to remember is that he considered this kind of approach regarding the teaching and parenting of children to be democratic. [1]

In 1981, Dr. Jane Nelsen wrote her book "*Positive Discipline,*" and from then to now, this notion has become more and more popular. But what does this concept actually means?

Well, it is based on the belief that there is no such thing as a bad child but only children who behave either in a good or bad way.

This method states that every child can be taught how to have a good behavior without hurting him/her in any way, verbally or physically.

However, this doesn't mean that a parent or a teacher who is using a positive discipline approach is ignoring the behavioral problems a child might have. This is the worst thing you can assume about the PD method.

So, the way to implement this concept is to actively participate in the process in which the child learns how to manage a situation. The key to success is that the adults involved need to remain friendly, calm, and respectful to the children throughout the way.

This being said, positive discipline incorporates more than one technique that will help parents to guide and control the behavior of their kids and will be very helpful for teachers who need to manage their students.

By applying this method, your children will learn how to make their own decisions, how to have expectations, and most importantly, they will also apply a positive behavior when interacting with other people. [2]

You might be thinking if there is also such a thing as a "*negative discipline*". So, not to leave you in the dark, let me tell you that, yes, this notion also exists, and as you can imagine, it is in the opposite direction from the positive one.

Not only that, negative discipline involves violent and angry responses and approaches that are fully forbidden when talking about PD, but also the options for reinforcing or punishing a child are very different.

For example, when talking about positive reinforcement, we can offer the child who behaved well a compliment to stimulate the repetition of that behavior. In contrast, negative reinforcement will mean to eliminate an undesired incentive.

As mentioned earlier, even punishment methods are very different. Yes, when choosing to educate a kid using positive discipline, punishments have to be applied. But can you correct a child without hurting his feelings and forbidding actions such as hanging out with friends or taking away his video games? Yes, you can.

Let's imagine that your child did something you specifically told him or her not to do, such as hurting a friend while playing. The right way to tackle the situation is not to prohibit any other encounter for a period of time with that friend or other friends for that matter but to make your kid apologize and understand that every action has repercussions.

In short, I want to repeat that the focus of the positive discipline is to set rational boundaries and to guide children in taking responsibility to respect them or discover how to handle the circumstances if they don't.

Before moving on and diving into the subject, I wish to take you through some statistics regarding the parent-child relationship. I am not doing this just for the sake of it but to make you realize the real situation of how adults are treating children worldwide.

Parenting Statistics

When it comes to parenting, usually, it doesn't really matter what kind of background the parents are coming from. In the end, all normal parents want more or less the same things for their children - to be healthy and have a good life.

This being said, it appears that regardless of the parents' education or social status, when it comes to parenting challenges or disciplining the children, the statistics say that most of them share the desire to have a well-behaved kid and also to be able to improve their parenting skills.

So, let's consider some statistics and try to understand what similarities can be seen in all parents and what characteristics are not very often observed.

Are you aware that more than 90% of mothers

and fathers believe that parenting is the biggest joy in their lives? Even though 73% of them say that the job of being a parent is the greatest challenge they ever encountered, almost the same percentage of people think that they started to really live only after the child came into their family.

Fascinating, right? Let's move on to more statistics. You might consider this information futile, but I truly think that knowing it will help you learn more about yourself as a parent. It will also make you realize in which category you fit and, therefore if you need to change anything about the way you are raising your child or if you are on the right track.

A crucial aspect that I want to present is that parents actually want to learn how to become better at this daily job. After studying multiple sources and surveys and also talking to parents from different backgrounds, I came to a very interesting conclusion.

Even though 80 percent of them consider

themselves to be good parents, more than 50% of the people that were surveyed wish they could be better. Moreover, almost 70 percent of the parents interviewed said that if they knew techniques and strategies of how to raise their children better, they would use them.

Since we are at this point, I wish to make a parenthesis. More than half of the parents do understand how important the 5 years of their child's life are, and this aspect terrifies them. Because of this, I feel obliged to discuss the topic a bit more.

Actually, the most important years of a child's life are the first 3 ones. [3] These years are the ones in which the brain's architecture is being built. To give you just a small anatomic example, during the first 3 years of life, every second of the day, the child's brain forms 700 neural connections.

This is why it is very important how the parents and other caretakers are interacting with the children. In the end, these, let's call them the first 1000 days of life, will turn your child into a better or a worse human being.

Therefore, kids that receive love and positive experience will grow up having more chances of having academic success and healthy relationships [4] than the ones that endure harsh caregiving. This later category of children tends to grow up and develop forms of depression, are more likely to start using drugs, and have bad human connections. [5]

But let's change the focus back to the subject of the book and see what statistics are available in the discipline area. Parents usually see discipline as a method to train their kids in such a way as to teach them to behave properly. However, not all parents use the same techniques, and we will get back to this subject in a few moments.

I will take the opportunity to say that statistically speaking, more than 60% of the parents not only see discipline as a way of nurturing their children but also as a protection form.

Even more significant is the fact that more than half of the parents wish to find the best way to teach their kids about discipline and even though some of them admit to raising their voice, 40% of them wish they didn't lose their temper so easily.

More and more parents have realized that negative discipline strategies, such as yelling or spanking, don't yield the best results when it comes to teaching a child to behave nicely. Even so, a big percentage of parents, 30% to be more precise, admit that they spank their kids even if they don't like doing it.

The good news is that even though there are a lot of parents that are using spanking as a technique to discipline their children, almost 80% of these parents realize that it is not such an effective method. Furthermore, more or less the same percentage of adults involved in caretaking are aware that yelling and calling names can be just as harmful as physical abuse for a child.

Children Statistics

For many years now, child abuse has been documented and studied. In fact, since the beginning of time, the violence against children, including mutilation, was reported even when looking back at the ancient civilizations. [6]

However, it was not until 1962 that this aspect was taken into real consideration by Kempe et al. in his seminary work known as "*The battered child syndrome.*"[7]

Today, we are well aware of the term "*battered*", but back then, it was a new expression that was used to describe the clinical indications of severe physical abuse when it comes to young children.

Even though four decades have passed, child

abuse is a problem more pressing than ever. It happens in more than one form, but I only want to talk about the subject of the book. This being said, let's check out some statistics that involve children abused as a form of discipline.

In 1995, an official survey was done in the United States of America, in which parents were asked how they discipline their children, and the results were not very promising. [8]

It appears that 49 children out of 1000 were victims of physical abuse when it comes to their discipline. These techniques included either hitting the child on the buttocks, hitting the child with an object, beating him/her and even if it's hard to imagine, many parents admitted to threatening their child with a gun or knife.

Before thinking that these atrocious discipline methods are happening only on the territory of the US, let me tell you that, yes, even though the physical abuse tends to be higher in the United States of America, other countries struggle with this issue as well. Because of this, I think it is really important to understand more, so let's take a look at some more data.

For example, in Egypt, more than 35% of children are reported being either tied up or beaten by their parents. More disturbing is that the figures state that 26% of these kids end up in the hospital with fractures, lose their consciousness, or even remain with permanent disabilities. [9]

Let's take another country example and talk about what happens in the Republic of Korea. More than a third of the parents surveyed admit to whipping their children as a form of discipline, and almost half of them talk about the fact of beating and hitting their offspring. [10]

But let's check out a European country and see how the situation is in this continent. A study made in Romania discovered that somewhere around 5% of the children are suffering from frequent and severe physical abuse. This harming of children not only involves hitting children regularly but also burning them and starving them.

However, regardless of the country, it appears that most of the children that are receiving a violent discipline usually receive hitting on the buttocks. Even though there are cases in which children are being choked, burned, or scared using a weapon, these situations are less frequent.

Even worse is the fact that these forms of violent discipline can even be seen in schools. This means that children can even suffer abuses in schools or kindergartens.

I won't continue on the matter because I am well aware that all this information is not very easy to digest. Therefore, let me switch to a happier tone and help you to try and understand if you are a good parent or are you doing something wrong.

CHAPTER TWO

HOW TO KNOW IF YOU ARE A GOOD PARENT

If you have one or more children and more importantly, if you are reading this book, you most likely want to know if you are doing everything right as a parent and if not, where are you failing.

The good news about modern parenting is that mothers and fathers around the world are wondering more and more if they are handling this non-stop daily job in the right way, so their babies can receive the best care.

Because of this, I want to take you on a short journey and offer you in this chapter the possibility to question yourself some vital questions. The only request I have from you is to think hard about them and only then answer yourself. The worst thing you can do is to compare yourself with other parents. Every family is special and different, so I advise you to continue reading to understand what is special about yours.

Question number 1: Does your child come to you when it has a problem or is hurting?

Think about the moments when your child has a problem. What does he or she do? Are you the person that your kid first calls for comfort? If the answer is a definite yes, you should know that you are doing something right.

It means that you have implemented a strong foundation that your child considers you the best place to return to when help is needed.

The best way to encourage your kid to continue doing so is to closely listen to his or her problems even if you consider them to be futile. After a closer listening, provide the best advice you can.

If you do this right, you will make your child open up and better communicate not only with you but also with others.

Question number 2: Does your child show its sentiments in front of you?

Handling the emotions of any person is not an easy task, but it is even more difficult when it comes to the emotions that your child is handling. Why? For multiple reasons. For example, you might not understand what is causing them, or they might come at the worst time for you.

Just as any human being, these small people, known as children, can also manifest sadness, joy, anger, and fear. The big question is: does your child trust you in such a way to express all these emotions?

The issue of children hiding feelings from their

parents is a very big problem that usually comes from the fact that parents are usually too busy to offer them the support they need when handling strong emotions.

The best approach would be to pay attention and show how much you appreciate and understand the feelings your child has. Teach your kid how to understand and handle its feelings. The worst action you can take is to shut your child down or distract him or her from the true feelings they are having at the time.

Question number 3: Is your feedback critical and labeling?

As a grownup, you know how bad it feels to be criticized and labeled, so be sure to treat your child in the same way. Of course, some feedback must be given from your side because otherwise, you cannot educate your kid. However, you need to teach yourself to do it in a nice and friendly manner.

Let's take an example so you can better

understand what I am trying to say. Think about those moments when you all sit at the table. Imagine what would you do if your child would take all the bread for himself/herself. How would you react?

Would you take the correct approach and teach him or her that sharing is an important part of being a good human being? Or would you do the most harmful thing and start calling names such as "*greedy*" or "*bad*"?

The most important part that you have to remember here is that feedback is critical, and even more important is the way you offer it. If you are not sure how you should handle this, just don't offer your kid a treatment that would humiliate even you as an adult.

Question number 4: Does your child feel comfortable in sharing their thoughts and feelings without worrying about your response?

This aspect is very important, and I will try to

explain in simple words why is that. First of all, if your kid is not afraid of how you will react, it is the best sign you can have that your parent-child relationship is an open and healthy one.

Unfortunately, there are many parents that unconsciously limit communication with their children due to their behavior. I am talking about those parents that are over-reacting to ideas or emotions that they don't like. Even more dangerous is the reaction some parents have when their behavior as a parent is being questioned.

In contrast, there are those parents who are so weak that even their children see them as fragile and keep their thoughts and feelings to themselves. This happens not because they are afraid of a bad reaction, but because they don't want to put an extra burden on their parents.

So, be sure that you are the rock of your child and not the other way around. Your kid needs the emotional support that only you as a parent can offer.

Question number 5: Do you create the right boundaries in order to keep your child safe?

I am 100% sure that you are aware that being a parent is not an easy task. However, being an awesome parent is probably the most difficult job in the world. But how can you turn from a normal parent into a rock star one?

You may not want to hear this, but the path to great parenting is paved with hard choices, such as setting the correct limits and boundaries that will guide your child's behavior and turn him or her into the best person he or she can become.

If a child is raised without any kind of boundaries, they usually grow up and have lots of problems working with others and living among people. However, if you set up the correct limits, your kid will grow up and will know how to love and appreciate what they have and will know how to earn not only money but also respect.

Of course, your child will probably hate some of the restrictions such as curfew hours or not being able to go to some parties, but it is your responsibility as a parent to be strict and explain why these boundaries exist for your child's sake and not your personal comfort.

Question number 6: Do you encourage your child to pursue their talents and interests?

If your child is too young to have specific interests, you will notice that as he or she will grow different abilities and start having interests in different aspects of life.

So, it is very important to help your child discover talents and passions. Even more essential is to support and encourage your kid to pursue their interests. This will surely let your children be able to engage with others during the teen and also during the young adult years.

As adults, we know how wonderful it is to feel the joy of success and excelling at something you love to do. Imagine that for a child, these feelings are augmented. This means that the joy a success that comes from achieving something great in a specific niche such as dancing or practicing a sport will mean a great deal for your child.

It will also teach your kid the taste of failure that comes along, and therefore, it will prepare the child for life.

However, as a parent, you should definitely don't put pressure on the child or to force a hobby. Children that do activities just for a parent's narcissistic ambition will end up hating that activity and will not be able to find their own path and talent.

This will only turn into a disappointment for both you as a parent and also for your child.

Question number 7: Do you repair the mistakes you do as a parent?

We all make mistakes, and we make them even as parents. This happens because there is no scientific path that, if you follow, you will be the best role model for your offspring.

Due to this, raising a child will imply taking steps that will not be the most excellent ones. Also, some of them will prove to be a mistake. However, you should not be worried about this. There is no perfect parent that never does or says something wrong.

The whole secret is how you handle those mistakes. Being capable of resolving relationship issues with your child is the best indication of being an awesome parent.

Let's take an example so you can really understand what I want to say. Imagine that your kid has done something that you disapprove of, and the first thing that you do is start yelling in frustration and disappointment. However, after a while, you realize that you could have handled the situation differently and feel bad about your reaction.

You can either shut your emotions and don't say anything, which I strongly don't recommend, or you can do what I do endorse, which is going to your child and explaining your feelings and also how you wished you have handled the situation.

By doing so, not only you will open up, and your kid will have the chance to know you better and understand that you are also just a normal human being that can make mistakes, but it will also improve your parenting skills.

Great! With that, your self-discovery is over. If you have read all these seven questions carefully and responded to them honestly, you probably know more about you as a parent and the relationship you have with your children than you did before.

I won't linger any longer on this subject because there are actually more pressing matters to discuss in this book, so let's move on and continue on the issue of discipline.

Daniel Faber

CHAPTER THREE

WHAT IS DISCIPLINE?

You might think that I should have started talking about discipline from the very beginning, but I wanted to clarify some aspects before doing so. I really believe that going through the statistics and your personal analysis will help you understand better what I will present next.

This being said, let's dig in and understand what discipline really is and how it affects the development of children. I will also guide you through and explain how the lack of discipline can affect a child for the rest of its life.

So, discipline is the action that is set to be in accordance with a precise method of governance. Discipline is usually used for improving human behavior. In the educational and professional worlds, discipline is a distinct part of knowledge, studying, or practice.

One of the concerns when it comes to both parents and teachers is to keep the children they are responsible for well-mannered. This is one method of being sure that they are learning how to behave to the fullest, but also be in a comfortable environment.

We all know that even when if we have the most civilized child, some sort of discipline is a necessity sometimes. Nevertheless, questions are advanced when it comes to discipline. Even psychoanalysts raise the topics of when is the time to be severe or where is the border of strictness drawn.

Let's start thinking about the meaning of the concept of *"misbehavior"*. Even as its name implies, misbehavior is the behavior that is regarded as improper for the setting or circumstances where it happens.

The first step is to clarify when a child actually acts inappropriately or misbehaves. There will be a full chapter on the subject, but still, some clarifications need to be made in order to continue this discussion.

So, we cannot universally say that if a kid interrupts you or a teacher while it is in the classroom, then that child is automatically rude. What if that child excuses before they interrupt? Then, why is it not considered a misbehavior?

So, in order to label a kid as offensive or not, you have to set up rules and regulations for him or her to follow. Also, indicate the behavior that you do not permit in your house or in the classroom, such as throwing food on the floor or not doing assignments.

There are many kinds of misconduct, and each of them needs a specific method or discipline scheme to be applied. The book "*Building Classroom Discipline: Sixth Edition*" [11] talks about the need for different kinds of discipline methods: preventive, supportive, and corrective. Let's take each one and see where it applies.

The **preventive discipline** concentrates on implementing a curriculum that is motivating, and that can grasp the attention of the children, making them focus on their tasks, especially their studies. By doing this, you, as an adult, will create a diversion for them. Therefore, they won't be able to misbehave. This includes displaying care and emotion to the children and recognizing their improvements.

The **supportive discipline** helps the children that are misbehaving with self-control. This method will assist them in getting back on track and requires showing enthusiasm in the child's work and presenting positive feedback and also aiding them when they are having difficulties.

Finally, the **corrective discipline** involves dealing directly with the problems. However, this should be done in such a way not to scare the children or make them feel uncomfortable.

Why it's Important to Discipline Your Child

If you think that discipline is just about teaching children that their actions have consequences, you are very wrong. Discipline ensures that they are learning the skills they will need to have when they grow up and turn into adults.

This being said, let's see why discipline is so important to be part of your child's life.

First of all, discipline will **help your kids to manage their anxiety**. Even though sometimes it is hard to believe, children don't have any desire to be in charge. Yes, they leave this impression from time to time, but studies have shown that they do it just to make sure that we, the parents or the teachers, can actually keep them protected.

Children who have parents that allow them too much may start having anxiety issues only because they have to make decisions designed to be taken by adults.

Yes, some children have anxiety problems without them being in the situation of making grown-up choices. Because of this, I think we should discuss this topic some more.

If we look at their nature, anxious children usually are sensitive and perfectionistic. Not only they desire to be the best version of themselves, but they also want you to be pleased with their actions. Due to this, disciplining restless children has its own difficulties. However, if it's done right, it can really help anxious and, of course, non-anxious kids. Not only they will turn out to be responsible adults, but you will also create a very strong bond between you two.

To do this correctly, discipline techniques should not be confused with punishment methods, even though often kids will perceive it as the same thing.

Discipline is more meaningful, more prolific, concentrating on teaching something, and not altering a behavior. It will make your child behave the way you want, but only because that behavior will start to make sense. Punishment, on the other hand, will develop a behavior but only because the child will fear consequences.

Keep in mind that discipline brings consequences when misbehaving but in a different way. Let's take an example to see exactly what I want to say.

Imagine that your kid has done something to upset you, such as not sharing their toys with their siblings. The correct way to discipline your child is to say, "*I am disappointed in you, and I thought I have raised you better*" and definitely not, "*You are grounded, so go in your room!*"

Another very important advantage that comes from discipline is that your kid will **learn how to make good choices**.

Before starting to question yourself how can

this be done, let me tell you that even though it is important for a child to have a routine in its daily program, it is more vital to allow him or her to make choices.

For instance, let's look at the moment of the morning in which your child has to eat breakfast and get ready for kindergarten or school every day. So, let him or her decide which one wants to be first. This way, your child will discover what morning routine they like best.

However, other examples are more harsh, even though they don't imply anything else than positive discipline. A very good example is when your kid plays ball in the middle of the street. You see that, and you take its ball, explaining how dangerous it is to play there. The child will make a connection between losing the playing privileges for a while and the risky road and will be able to make a safer choice for a playground next time.

Healthy discipline shows kids more than one way to get their necessities satisfied. Children have to discover problem-solving and self-regulation abilities from proper training.

Let me repeat this. It is essential to create a difference between punishments and consequences. If kids are disciplined with suitable consequences, it will help them learn from their errors.

You might think that this information is redundant, but yes, **discipline will keep your children safe**. What better way to be sure that your child is protected than to teach him or her primary safety rules such as keeping their hand away from fire or looking both directions before crossing the road?

But this is not all. Teaching your child that eating too many sweets is not good for health will prevent diseases such as diabetes or obesity. If you allow your kids to eat whatever they want, they might have to face serious health problems. This is why it is essential to establish healthy boundaries and provide guidance to assist your child in learning how to make good choices when it comes to their well-being.

As you can imagine doing it right so, your child will actually listen to you is no walk in the park. You have to explain the underlying motivations for your rules in such a way that your kid will understand the protection problems.

Let's take an example. So, your kid refuses healthy food such as vegetables and only eats cookies. If you forbid him or her to eat sweets, you will only make your child hide those and eat them anyway. However, if you explain the health risks and how eating only desserts will make them sick, you will most probably have more success in making them accept a balanced meal.

If your kid learns about the logic behind your disciplinary rules, he or she will also learn the particular safety risks. By doing so, the child will be more inclined to recognize them when you are not around to advise them what to do.

To be sure this works, make it so that for every rule, you let the value behind it to be known. Explain the importance as much as you can without sounding too pressing.

Last, but not least, disciplining your children will teach them how to **deal with their emotions**. For example, if your kid throws a toy in anger on one of their siblings or friends, of course, you need to explain how that gesture is not nice. However, you should also give him or her some time alone. Yes, the child will consider solitude a punishment, but it will also offer the chance to learn how to manage anger and emotions in the future.

Ignoring mild misbehavior can teach kids socially appropriate ways to manage their frustration as well. If you refuse to give in to a temper tantrum, your child will learn that's not a good way to get his needs met. When you ignore whining, your child will learn that this kind of action from their side won't change your behavior.

The only thing that you should keep in mind is that when your kid is going through intense emotions, you will also feel them, and I should not be the one to tell you that in these times, we are not very full of wisdom or problem-solving ideas. Because of that, I recommend not trying to make your point then. If you do so, you will only make things worse.

Just let your kid know that you are there and that you understand their distress but in such a way that they won't believe that you agree with them or even worse that you are supporting their behavior.

Use words such as, "*I am aware that you are angry right now, but you should not behave like that.*" This way, you let them know that you are strong and the person in charge but also gentle and loving.

Remember that when kids are out of control,

they don't do it to be manipulative; they simply do it because they want something that they don't get. Finding out what is that your child wants in order to calm him or her down is not always an easy job, simply because the child doesn't always know what it lacks. Think about how hard it is to reason with your child when they are lacking sleep. Kids will never admit that they need to rest, but they are really impossible little "*creatures*" when are tired.

This is the reason why it is crucial to let your kid have their space. Only by doing so you will teach him or her discipline and also how to handle their emotions.

Effects of Lack of Discipline

As you could probably already noticed, the reason why discipline needs to be part of our children's life is not only good for the way they behave, but it is also essential for how they grow up. Yes, without a discipline method, kids will grow up without knowing how to handle relationships or overpass life challenges.

Even if it is hard to believe, the truth is that even as children, kids who don't receive a disciplined routine are not happy. Actually, this is the reason why we see so many angry kids these days. So many parents consider that they need to spend more time working to raise money than disciplining their offspring, and the results are not pleasant.

I want to talk about the need and also the ways to teach your kid how to behave based on its age, but before that, let's find out what are the repercussions of not disciplining your child.

You might ask what kind of parent doesn't want to have a well-behaved kid. Well, actually, there are many motives for doing so. For example, there are cases in which parents prefer not to educate their children properly for silly reasons such as not upsetting the kids, while others are so busy with their work that they simply don't have time to spend teaching their infants.

Of course, there are also those cases in which parents have really bad memories of how they were disciplined when they were young, so they just refuse to do anything to teach their babies how to behave from fear of them not growing up with the same trauma.

It doesn't matter what is the reason for which parents don't discipline their kids. What does matter is the results to be the same. Child discipline, especially when it's done right, is not about seeking control over your child but about teaching them how to manage their own behavior.

But what is the outcome of a lack of discipline? Many signs can be noticed in grownups that represent a deficient discipline during the youth years, such as selfishness, bad relationships, substance abuse, and lack of empathy. All these can translate into an unhappy life. Let's talk about the most frequent consequences that can appear in children that don't receive a good discipline.

First of all, kids that don't receive the proper education and control will develop **antisocial behaviors**. But what does "*antisocial*" means? Based on Berger's book [12], anti-social behavior is represented by actions that can harm the well-being of other people.

This way of acting mostly occurs within social interaction in the family and society. It influences a child's personality, cognitive capacity, and engagement with negative peers, dramatically altering children's problem-solving abilities. [13]

A severe form of antisocial behavior can be the reason for substance abuse that can lead to health problems and even crime. Therefore, poor parenting, like the lack of discipline, can lead to drug use, domestic violence and depression. This is also observed in children who come from abusive families.

Another issue that can arise when children don't receive a good discipline is that they develop **poor resilience**. Let's see what that represents, but to understand this notion, we need to talk a little about what psychological resilience represents. It is the capacity to mentally and also emotionally cope with a problem. [14]

This being said, resilience can be seen in people who develop behavioral capacities, which permit them to remain calm during crises and to surpass the incident.

Without the help of proper discipline, kids cannot learn how to cope with emotional and physical trauma. In this situation, poor parenting appears in the body of not shielding the infant from a bad situation or not being capable of managing negative sentiments, all of which affect the child.

Moving on, researchers have concluded that children who don't receive a proper discipline tend to develop **forms of depression**.

Of course, it is normal for kids to sometimes

feel sad or irritated. However, if the negative feelings remain for a lengthy period, and it doesn't let your child act like a normal kid, it might be a case of depression. I am sure that you know what depression is and how dangerous it is, but I want to take a minute to define just in case some readers don't comprehend what I am talking about.

Depression is a mood disorder. When talking about children's depression, the foremost symptom is sadness, but it can also be long-termed irritability. It can intervene with their energy, attention, rest, and appetite, all these resulting in lack of interest in any kind of activities or social encounters.

This kind of depression can be undetected and can come to the surface after many years when a very severe form of illness may occur. These kinds of situations can end with self-harm and even suicide.

However, all these can be avoided if the child

receives good care and discipline while growing up.

When kids don't receive an appropriate discipline, they can even become **aggressive**. But how exactly can a kid be aggressive? Let's look into more depth in this issue.

Aggression in children can be a sign of various underlying issues. It is a combination of psychiatric conditions and life circumstances. For example, toddlers can act aggressively sometimes only because they lack the verbal abilities to get what they need. [15]

Imagine two kids that don't know how to talk very well. I will call them John and Jack. So, John and Jack are playing together, and John takes one of Jack's toys. Jack cannot express his frustration using words, so he becomes aggressive towards him.

Of course, with the proper discipline, this behavior can be corrected if you teach your child how aggression is not the way to solve the issue. Usually, this kind of behavior is gone after the child grows up and learns how to communicate.

However, if this kind of treating others extends to school years, then the situation is not to be ignored.

Many pieces of research have shown that children who have real violence issues ordinarily have a bad relationship with their parents, especially mothers. Therefore negative parenting methods such as severe treatment and displaying cold sentiments towards the child throughout childhood will make the child have high levels of anger.

Another great issue that can be born after a precarious discipline is the **lack of empathy**. If we consider this for a while, empathy is one of our core characteristics that make us human. It is our connection to others. It is what lets us feel the emotions of others.

When compassion is missing, then extreme

mental issues may occur. Of course, many mental disorders have a genetic correlation, but even if such an inheritance exists or not, the childhood environment and possible traumas from these years are extremely important.

The most common psychological diseases that come from the lack of empathy are psychopathy and sociopathy. I don't want to get more into this issue, because this is not the topic of the book, but I think it is very important that you understand the risks of not providing good discipline.

So, if the child is handled with indifference by the parents, the odds of treating others the same are highly increased. But if the child receives love and understanding, while learning the differences between right and wrong, he or she will develop the abilities to care about other people.

The last result of the lack of discipline I want to talk about is probably the most straightforward - **having a hard time with relationships**.

This happens especially in cases in which a child receives love and understanding only when it does something to make the parent happy. Because of this, the child will learn that love is actually a conditional aspect, and the meaning of "*unconditional love*" doesn't really exist.

If they grow up in this kind of environment, they will not understand love and will see any kind of affection as being suspicious and odd, therefore, most probably, all the future relationships as an adult will turn into failure.

Unfortunately, the lack of good, healthy relationships goes hand in hand with another very important issue known as **low self-confidence**.

Just think about it. If a child is raised hearing every day how worthless he or she is, not only they will not understand the meaning of genuine love, but they will also grow up to believe that they don't have any value to give to the world.

CHAPTER FOUR

THE CORRECT WAY TO DISCIPLINE A CHILD BASED ON AGE

I previously promised you to dedicate a whole chapter on the subject of how to apply discipline techniques based on each age period of your child.

Yes, it doesn't matter how old your kid is. Each life part requires some teaching, and the discipline you give must be consistent.

Before starting the guideline, I want to tell you about the most important aspect you need to understand. If you, as a parent, don't stick to the rules and values that you set up, your children won't do it either.

But, let's take each period of your child's life of which you are fully responsible to mold and see what are the correct ways to approach him or her and how to teach them to become the best version of themselves.

I advise you to read the full chapter even if your child has already passed an age interval. This way, you will be able to reflect on how you acted in that period, and if some changes in your approach can still be made.

Newborn to 2 Years Old

This is the time in which the babies discover the world, and with this discovery comes the curiosity and the desire to know more. During this period, the brain is exactly like a sponge that absorbs all the information surrounding them.

Because of this, the best thing you can do is eliminate attractions that can be dangerous such as jewelry, medicine, or cleaning products, which can be ingested and produce harm. Also,

I know that parents prefer leaving the child in front of a TV and do their house chores, but I highly advise the contrary. Video equipment at this age is just as toxic for the brain as chemical products are for the stomach.

Of course, crawling babies will tend to put their hands on unacceptable objects. The simplest way to solve this is to simply but calmly say, "*No*". The worst thing you can do is to rush the child and yell at him or her. After gently saying "*No*", try and distract the child with an appropriate activity. As I've said, at this age, they are really curious, so a shiny suitable toy will captivate them and they will forget about the forbidden gadget.

On the other hand, timeouts can also be a form of useful discipline for toddlers. As I previously mentioned, when kids cannot verbally communicate, they tend to become aggressive to make a point. Explain to your child how this kind of behavior is not acceptable and give him and her two minutes of a timeout to calm down.

Whatever you do, don't spank your child. At this age, the child will not make the connection between punishment and their actions. However, they will imitate you since you are their role-model and will tend to be even more offensive towards you and other kids.

From 3 to 5 Years Old

Your child is growing up very fast in this timeframe, and they start to understand more and more about life. Also, because during this interval, the child accumulates so much information, she or he will start making connections between their actions and the consequences that come from them. Due to this, it is the best time to start explaining the house rules.

So, it is important that you talk to your kid and explain the differences between right and wrong, how it is ok to behave, and what is forbidden.

For example, starting with the age of 3,

whenever your child does something that you disagree with, such as throwing food on the floor, try not to yell. Remain calm and explain how wasting food is not acceptable in your house. Also, think of a suitable consequence for this action, like telling your kid that the next time he or she does something like that, they will have to clean the mess.

The sooner you establish rules, the better it is for everybody. I know that sometimes it is hard to always express your dissatisfaction, but overlooking the violation of your own rules will not help your child grow up and turn into the person you want him or her to become. Empty threats will weaken your authority as a mother or father, and your kid will just test your limits.

The only thing that you should not forget about is that good deeds also have consequences, so be sure to offer your child a reward for every positive action. Tell your baby how proud you are of him or her with every occasion, but don't forget to specify the part of their behavior that satisfied you. By doing so, it is more probable for your child to repeat the gesture only to make you happy. This way, it will become a habit and will come to them naturally.

Of course, disciplining some kids will be an easier job than others. If you have a very stubborn kid with a very strong personality, you will need to try some other techniques. For example, give your kid a timeout whenever it does something bad. Be sure you send your kid to contemplate the things that have upset you, somewhere without distractions such as a TV or computer.

The most important thing when giving a kid a timeout is to not offer him or her any kind of attention. Don't talk to them, don't look at them, and don't give them any impressions that you are about to forgive them.

There is no exact time of how long the timeout should be. Try multiple time intervals and see what works for your child. Researchers say that for each year of life, you should add a minute, but again, you need to test and see what length is suitable for your case.

The last thing I want to talk about when it comes to disciplining a toddler is the necessity of giving clear commands, which are also self-explanatory when it comes to distinguishing right from wrong.

From 6 to 8 Years Old

This represents the period of time in which your child starts going to school and becomes more and more responsible for their life. Because of this, the education you give is very important, so let's see how you should act and how you shouldn't.

Even though your kid is older and knows more about what he or she likes or dislikes, it is still important to keep your rules standing and apply the necessary consequences.

Timeouts are still very effective, so don't be afraid to make use of them. One important thing is to always be consistent. It is very important that your child actually believes what you are saying. To be sure that your kid takes you seriously, don't start making unrealistic threats such as, "*Do your homework or you will not play PlayStation ever again in your life.*" Both of you know that this will not happen, so the child will just ignore you.

Lastly, remember that you are raising a child and not starting a military school. So, give your child not only the benefit of the doubt but also a second chance when he or she makes a mistake.

From 9 to 12 Years Old

You will notice that even though kids are growing up, it will not become easier to discipline them. However, if you follow the golden rule of natural consequences, then you should be able to educate your offspring without issues.

You will see that as they grow, they evolve and

become more mature. With this, they will start requesting more freedom and trust. So, what you need to do is to teach them how to deal with the results of their behavior. By doing so, you will ensure an efficient and suitable method of discipline.

I propose to take an example and see exactly what I am talking about. Let's say that your kid has broken one of the school's windows, and you are called to the principal's office to discuss the issue. An inappropriate thing you can do is to rescue your kid from detention and not let him or her take the blame.

By letting your kid take the punishment, you will help him or her to learn a very important life lesson. They will learn that bad actions bring hard consequences, and even more importantly, they will acknowledge the fact that you, as a parent, won't always be there to save them.

Only by learning from their own mistakes, they

will be able to keep themselves away from similar situations.

If you see that natural consequences don't have any effect on your child, remember that this age period is the best to use interdictions on electronic devices as a consequence of their actions.

Teenage Years

I consider this period to be the most difficult one because, during these years, your baby is no longer a child per se. They have their own desires and expectations and probably know what they want to do with their life. However, during these years, your child needs you just as much because they can make some very big mistakes that they will regret for the rest of their life. So, I advise you to pay great attention to what I have to say next.

Until now, you already gave them the basis of the education they need in order to have a good life. Your kid is aware of what is good and what are the aspects of life that should stay away from. Yet, they still need your rules and guardianship more than ever.

Therefore, set up boundaries even though most probably your child will hate them. Too much independence will not be good for your child, just as too much limitation will not prepare them for life.

This being said, let your kid have friends and go to parties, but be sure that those friends are not a bad influence, and curfew hours are set.

Don't forbid your child to date. It will just make them do it behind your back and do stupid things. Let them discover the meaning and implications of a relationship. Let your child know that you will always have an ear for their problems and a shoulder for him or her to cry on.

Most importantly, don't be afraid to talk about the sexual aspects of life. This is exactly the age period when people are discovering their sexuality and become curious about their bodies. Talk to them about how starting their sex life is a very big deal and how they should wait for the right time and person. Explain to them the importance of protection and about the risks of contracting a disease or an unwanted pregnancy.

Even if your child will not feel very comfortable talking to you about these aspects, they need to know that you are open to discussion.

So, to wrap this part up, it is really important to establish the appropriate limits for your child at this age. The relationship you will have with your child will be influenced by this age period.

Last but not least, raising a teenager is not about control. It is about focusing on the positive aspects to help your kid discover their life path.

CHAPTER FIVE

POSITIVE DISCIPLINE APPROACH

This book is about positive discipline, so I think that it is very important to talk more about this exact topic. Therefore, this chapter will be the longest one you will read, so I suggest you find time to focus on it carefully.

Since it is such a sensitive and easy to misinterpret subject, I will try to give you as many examples as possible. Also, I will try to describe everything in easy to understand words, so that every parent out there who owns a copy can fully understand what I am about to say. So let's start!

Criteria for Positive Discipline

Firstly, I will tackle the subject of the principles

behind this discipline technique. These principles are known all over the world as the five criteria for effective positive discipline. [16] I want to be sure that you really understand them, so let's take each of them at a time and go into the core of each criterion.

Criterion number 1. It helps children feel a sense of connection- belonging and significance

I want to return to Alfred Adler because he was one of the first that stated that we, as humans, are pulled towards a feeling of belonging and significance.

But what does that actually mean, and why do we want it for our kids? I will start with the notion of *"belonging"* and move to *"significance"* from there.

So, the idea of *"belonging"* is actually about how people connect and fit in bigger groups, regardless if we talk about their family, school, or workplace. Therefore, this is most definitely something we want our kids to accomplish. We don't them to be outcasts and feel unwanted when entering a room.

Positive discipline not only will help them to find a place where they truly fit, but it will also let them realize when the connection they have with some people starts to alter and will help them decide whether to try and fix it or to find a more appropriate group.

Moving on, let's go to "*significance*". This refers to how we can contribute to the world. So, what does that mean, and how can we quantify it?

It is about how the things we do matter on a larger scale. It is known that people who think that they give something meaningful to society tend to be happier. This is true simply because they acknowledge that what they do makes a difference. According to this theory, we want our children to feel that their life matters, and they can change the way the world progresses.

This is why positive discipline is such a good

approach to educate children. It allows them not only to learn how to behave but also how to turn into a successful exponent of the generation they represent.

Kids are born with talents but not with skills. This is why it is important to encourage them to find their own path. By doing so, not only will they find the domain in which they can matter but also groups in which they belong.

Even more vital is the way parents react to the moments when children feel discouraged or make mistakes when trying to integrate. I will give you an example to understand what I am talking about.

Let's imagine that your family just moved into a new city, and your kid finds it hard to make new friends at school. If you also start to criticize him or her, you will make your child feel like they do not belong there. So, instead of analyzing their grades and the lack of desire to go to the new school, spend some special time with your kid and explain to him or her how amazing they are and how they can do great things.

Remember that a child who is introverted and hurting will most probably try and hurt others just so it won't feel alone, and you don't want that.

The best approach in that situation is to take small steps and to encourage your child in their positive actions. If you do it right, you will be able to bring that child back to the point of significance and belonging.

Children are learning each day about belonging and significance, and sometimes it is really hard for adults to keep track of the changes their offspring are living. However, you should keep in mind that it is your job to guide them and put them back on the right track when they feel lost. And there is no better way to do so then to use positive discipline as a means to an end.

Criterion number 2. It is mutually

respectful and encouraging - kind and firm at the same time

The other father of the positive discipline, Dr. Drekurs talks about how important it is to treat your child with both firmness and kindness. As you can imagine, being kind is a very important factor when educating children, mostly because it will set up an example of how to treat others.

On the other hand, being a firm parent is just as essential when raising a child. This will not only make your kid take you seriously and follow your rules but it will also teach them that in order to receive respect, you have to be very determined.

This being said, it is clear as day why kindness and firmness are essential parts of positive discipline. However, when it comes to putting this part of the education into actual actions, both parents and teachers don't find it very easy.

First of all, it is not really in our human nature

to be kind when somebody is getting on our nerves. This is why it is recommended for adults, just as much as it is for children, to take timeouts and calm down. Only by doing this, you will be able to treat your kid in a kind matter even when you are really angry with their actions.

The other very great issue in the kindness approach that positive discipline recommends is that there is always the risk of becoming too permissive simply because you don't want to be too strict and disciplinary.

A very great number of parents wrongly consider that if they offer a very tolerant life to their children, they will not learn what disappointment means. That is the worst thing you can do. Not only that, this doesn't have anything to do with kindness, but it will also not prepare your child in any way for life. And we all know that life is all about disappointments.

But then, what is kindness when educating a

child? In the process of disciplining a kid, you have to show respect for both you and your offspring. It means that you have to validate their feelings without pampering them. It also means to teach your kid that respect is a mutual aspect of your parent-child relationship.

Of course, the theory is so much easier than putting it into practice. The tricky part comes when you have to implement some consequences for bad actions.

Punishment is disrespectful, right? So, then how can you handle such a situation?

Give yourself and your kid some timeout. By doing so, you will not let the child get away with whatever they have done, but it will give you both the time to contemplate how to approach the situation in the best possible terms. By doing so, neither of you will say something that you later regret.

The next aspect I want to teach you is how to be firm and kind at the same time. Yes, many people misinterpret firmness with some kind of punishment but remember that this is why positive discipline considers kindness and firmness to be a whole. When combined, the two of them can only lead to a single characteristic - respect.

So, be sure to keep the firm attitude when setting up boundaries. Set up limits that are reasonable and stick to them. In the end, limits are there only to keep your child safe. By introducing fair and firm boundaries, your child will not feel the need to break them, and you will keep him or her safe.

My advice to you is that as your kid grows, make the limits together. Talk about what the child considers reasonable and what you feel like it is important. Meet somewhere in the middle. We were all kids and especially teenagers and know how unfair almost every decision made by our parents felt like.

If you ever feel trapped and don't know what

words to use, try sentences such as, *"I know that you can be respectful, so why don't you try it?"* or *"Go to your room and we will talk later about this"*.

Criterion number 3. It is effective long-term - consider what the children are thinking, feeling, learning, and deciding about themselves and their world and what to do in the future to survive or to thrive

The best form of discipline is the one that shows results in the long-term. When you educate your child, you want him or her to remember what you teach them in the future and not only for a few days. Ever since your baby is born, you have to adopt passive discipline. Even if you don't realize, actually adopting a daily schedule of sleeping, playing, or eating, is the first step that you need to implement for a successful form of positive discipline.

This is true because biologic rhythms usually become a regularity, and therefore, the child will adapt to your family customs. Signals of distress, such as crying, are transformed as children begin to remember how their pain and suffering have been relieved and discover new approaches to make parents pay attention to their emerging needs. [17]

As they are growing up and turn from toddlers into preschoolers, children's needs become more and more diverse and therefore, the discipline has to be more versatile.

Luckily, positive discipline is the technique you need in order to offer an appropriate education for complex physical and social environments. It lets you develop creative tactics to guard them and guide them in desirable patterns of behavior. At preschool age, kids start to acquire a perception of rules. By doing so, their behavior is controlled by these rules and, of course, by the consequences correlated to them.

When they reach school age, all the rules that you have established all years before have to turn into an increasing sense of responsibility and self-discipline.

As they grow, positive discipline will help you do a natural and gradual transfer of responsibility from you to your child. This will be most visible starting with the teenage years.

Adolescence is not an easy period for either of the parties involved. However, if you do this right and practice a proper positive discipline from the moment your baby is born, you will be able to help your child during their biggest life transition.

Criterion number 4. Teaches

important social and life skills - respect, concern for others, problem-solving, cooperation and the skills to contribute to the home, school, or larger community

When people think about discipline, usually they imagine it is a technique used only to reduce unwanted behaviors. Yet, this couldn't be more wrong. Education is also about increasing desirable actions just as much. This is why a positive approach is more and more recommended by specialists, and I will tell you exactly why.

Reducing unacceptable behavior without having a plan to stimulate a more pleasing one is not effective, and therefore, it is not desirable.

What positive discipline does is to take the riskiest part of training children, such as teaching them habits that meet parental expectations, while also promoting healthy social relationships. More so, it assists them in growing a form of self-discipline that will transform into positive self-esteem.

The truth is that many helpful behavioral models develop as part of the child's normal evolution. So, then what is the role of the parents in this equation? Their part, which is a vital one, is to see these behaviors and give the correct feedback to encourage and cultivate them.

However, this is not all adults have to do. Parenting is not an easy task, and other desirable behaviors are not part of a child's fundamental way of being and therefore require teaching. These actions include elements such as good manners, the ability to share with others, the desire to study, developing social relationships and last, but definitely not least, empathy.

With the help of positive behavior, kids can learn all of the above without waiting for quick rewards for how they act.

You might wonder at this point what approach to take to teach your kids how to act positively towards others. Each parent needs to find their own way to get to their child. However, if you provide regular positive attention and listen carefully to what he or she has to say, reinforce your child's decisions and talk about how important it is to be kind to others, you have a great place to start.[18]

Such approaches have several advantages. First of all, the wanted behavior has better chances of becoming internalized, and the recently discovered behavior will be a foundation for other positive habits. Furthermore, the emotional climate of your family will be pleasant and, of course, supportive.

Criterion number 5. It motivates children to discover how capable they are and encourages the constructive use of personal power and autonomy

The fifth positive discipline criterion concerns

how parenting can facilitate self-regulation in children. But what does a self-regulation behavior truly mean? If we are to look at the actual definition, self-regulated actions are those that are initiated by each person and include a feeling or practice of self-determination. In this application of the concept, *"self"* refers not only to the physical form but to the experiential self and activities that are recognized as one's own.

One approach to describe the field of personal power and autonomy is to differentiate it from other areas displaying positive child consequences. In this case, the most pertinent is compliance. You probably are aware of what compliance means, but I want to make a short stop here and talk for a second about this notion and give an example.

In simple words, compliance is the space to which children respond quickly to what you tell them to do. So, compliance concerns to a particular directive, demand, or rule to be followed. On the other hand, self-regulation concerns if children start to behave appropriately, even if they are not explicitly asked.

Let's take a case to see the difference between the two. If you tell your child to clean their room and he or she does as you've asked, then we can talk about compliance. But, if your kid cleans their room without any indication, we are the witness of a self-regulating behavior.

It is redundant to say that, of course, what you want from your kid is to learn how to act on their own and take actions and decisions based on what they think has to be done and not on your demands.

This is the reason why it is so important to use a correct positive discipline approach. Only by providing the correct example of how to behave and set normal and healthy house rules, your child will be able to grow up and become a self-regulating and self-sufficient human being.

The Core of Positive Discipline

Even when looking at an aspect from a scientific point of view, the secret of acknowledging all of its mysteries is looking into its core. Because of this, I propose to *"cut"* into the notion of positive discipline and see what its nucleus has to offer.

1. None of the kids are bad; they just have bad behavior.

Every good children therapist will tell you that when a toddler is acting out, it should not be considered a motive for punishment. More so, you should be very careful about your child's needs because these actions are usually a cry for attention.

This being said, it is normal behavior for a toddler and can be translated into the core sentence we are discussing now *"There are no bad kids, just bad behavior"*. So, when do these acts turn into issues?

The problems begin when the child starts to test your boundaries and starts behaving this way even though they don't have any reason for doing so. If you keep changing the limits and permit your child too much, you will not help him or her in any way. You will not show any signs of kindness. Instead, you will neglect your kid and their education.

The solution for a good and efficient discipline is our approach. These years of toddlerhood are the best ones to sharpen your parenting abilities, which will contribute to the honest and compassionate guidance our children will depend on for years to come. [19]

I will give you a very clear example for you to understand how you should react and how you should most definitely not. Let's say that you are in a mall, and your kid starts screaming and throwing his or her toys at you. In this case, most probably, the first feelings you have are the embarrassment and frustration.

The worst approach you can have in this case is to use expressions such as "*bad child*". By doing so, you will augment the negative picture of your son or daughter, in both your own mind and their own.

However, if you, as a parent, understand that your child might just be hungry or tired and accept that your kid is not bad but only the way they behave at that moment is not acceptable, it will be very beneficial for their education.

So, instead of yelling at him or her things such as "*How can you behave in such a way?*", you should try and say, "*We don't throw our toys because we can hurt somebody with them.*"

If you keep your calm and explain the positive parts that come from your child not acting in a bad way, you will make him or her understand that they are good kids that just need a different behavior when their body has a need, regardless if it's food or rest.

2. Don't just point out the wrong behavior; show them how to set things right.

The next part of the positive discipline's core is linked to the previous one and goes beyond toddlerhood. This bullet point is all about setting a good example for your child to follow. Also, it is about pointing out a positive aspect of a gesture and not the negative ones.

If you simply forbid your kid to behave unacceptably without explaining why you find that approach undesirable, you will just receive a momentarily result. Your child needs to understand why some actions are forbidden and what are the direct consequences of their behavior concerning other people.

So, if you are in a situation in which the child does something wrong, it is not recommended to use expressions such as *"Don't do that!"*

Why? Because your child doesn't understand your motivation. If you don't explain the logic,, the infant will likely do the exact same thing in a similar situation.

Imagine that you have two kids. If one of them steals the candy from his or her sibling, the best approach is to explain why it is important in life to know how to share and why stealing is a bad habit.

There are situations in which simply highlighting the positive aspects of a reason is not enough. My recommendation for these cases is to try the positive parenting tool known as "*time in*".

What makes it different from the "*time out*" method is that in opposed to sending the child to sit alone in a chair or in a corner, this strategy advises that the child be taken in a private space with their caregiver and is encouraged to talk freely about their feelings until finally cools down.

Throughout the time-in period, parents should empathize with the kid's emotions. However, this should not be mistaken with permitting your child to continue with inappropriate behavior. The great advantage of a time-in is that it allows you to really connect and approach whatever behavior change has to be made.

The reason why this procedure works is that often children need reassurance that their needs are being considered. Also, if you offer your child a time-in, you will teach him or her how to express their feelings, and they will not feel isolated such as when they are sent into time-outs.

3. Be kind but firm; exhibit empathy and respect.

It is very hard to have a contradictory discussion with a kid. In their minds, children probably don't see any issue in the way they act. Furthermore, just as every person considers themselves right, infants also think of themselves to be right and justified. This behavior can turn into something very frustrating for you and you might end up having a bad approach to solve the issue.

Just imagine your kid hitting a friend and then giving an explanation such as, "*He started it.*" I know that this can hit a nerve, especially after a long day. But as a parent, rather than arguing with your kid and turning the situation into a never-ending story, you should just stay calm and explain everything you have to say.

Being calm but firm will not only bring more success in your argument, but it will also help you show some empathy. Just by empathizing with your child and understanding how he or she really wants the toy that started the conflict, you can win half the battle.

I want us to talk a little more about this topic because I really think it is one of the most important parts of the discipline.

In the book "*Positive Discipline for Preschoolers*", the authors talk about how being kind and firm when these kinds of situations happen can be easier if you apply some prevention. [20]

The first step is to understand why your child was motivated in the first place to exhibit unwanted behavior. Was your kid hungry or sleepy? Most probably, everything could have been avoided with just a little prevention from your side.

However, if this would be so easy, we would all have model children and would be the best parents. But the real world works differently, and even with the prevention approach, your kid will still misbehave from time to time.

For these moments, there is nothing else you can do than to act firm and kind. The most challenging task you will have is not to become either too permissive or use excessive control. No good will come from either of these behaviors.

Remember to stay calm and firm and, most importantly, acknowledge the fact that there is no perfect parent or child. We all make mistakes, but it helps to be conscious of the many slips that can be made in the name of love. Only after doing so, you will be able to correct the mistakes once they have been made. [20]

4. Whenever possible, offer choices.

I always think that if people are allowed to make their own choices, they can learn from their own experience and therefore actually understand why some actions are good while others are bad.

Positive discipline works in the same way, but of course, since we are educating children, and they need to be taught the difference between right and wrong, these choices need to be limited.

Allowing limited options rather than making demands can be very useful. Children usually give a favorable response when they are given the possibility of choice, especially when they hear the expression "*You decide.*" However, choices need to be carefully offered and should force them to concentrate on the needs of the situation.

These choices are directly correlated to responsibility. Therefore, infants should receive more limited choices than older children. I will give you a full example so you can understand exactly what I am trying to say.

Let's say you have two children. The girl is 3 years old, and the boy is 10. When you prepare to go to the park, you prepare two dresses for your daughter to choose from, while you let your son take full responsibility for his clothing choice.

Remember that you cannot give multiple choices if you, as an adult, don't accept them all.

Don't offer a solution for your child if you don't agree with it. Don't ask, "*Do you want to eat broccoli or pizza?*" if you are not happy with your child eating junk food. If you want your kid to eat the veggies, make it sound like something fun and give multiple healthy choices such as, "*Today, you decide if we are having carrot sticks or roasted sweet potatoes.*"

By doing so, you let them know that there is no say on the matter of eating vegetables, but the child will eat it happier since they made the choice.

5. Treat mistakes as opportunities to learn.

There is no one who never makes a mistake. Thus, since kids are nothing more and nothing less than small human beings, they also make mistakes from time to time. The best thing you can do in this case is to use these moments not to punish your child but as an opportunity to teach him or her the right way to behave.

I am well aware that parents have the best intentions even when they react negatively, but unfortunately, this kind of response doesn't motivate the children in any way. This means that the next similar situation will occur, the children will probably not act any different.

Education needs to be about anything but fear. It has to be about setting examples and teaching the child to act in the right way. And what better way to do so other than using their own mistakes to explain why they should not behave in that manner.

When you educate your kid, don't think more of what others have to say about your methods; think about what your child is actually learning from their mistakes. It is equally bad to humiliate your child in the hope that he or she will learn to be afraid of the possible embarrassment and won't repeat the gesture.

The correct way to behave when your child makes a mistake is to motivate the kid to make better choices without paying the price of low self-esteem or physical pain.

For instance, when your son or daughter lies about a grade and you are called at school after a few days to talk to the teacher about it, the worst thing you can do is yell at your child. The correct way is to discuss the reason for lying. Therefore, instead of saying, *"You are grounded! I cannot believe you got an F and worse that you made me make a fool of myself in front of your teacher,"* you can use a different approach such as *"It is not good that you've lied to me, but let's both take a moment and understand where we failed - you lying to me and me making you fear my reaction."*

Kids need to know that adults also make mistakes, and everybody has to learn from them regardless of age. By doing this, you will be able to have an open relationship with your offspring.

6. Make changes in the situation - prevent the misbehavior from being repeated.

We have talked about how prevention has a real effect and how it can simplify a lot of work when it comes to educating children. Now, I want to focus on another technique known as redirection. It is also known as changing the scene and it is as beautiful as it is simple to apply.

So, this distraction means offering your child an alternative for their activity to avoid potential problems that can be caused by its current one. Maybe the definition is not the easiest one to understand, but don't worry because I have some examples for you that you will make light on the matter.

However, before moving on and talking about real-life cases, I want to highlight that this approach can be used for many age periods: early infancy, toddlers, and preschoolers. After the child reaches school age, you will see that redirection is not so effective anymore. Why? The explanation is very simple. Younger children have a short attention span and this is a characteristic that you should take advantage of.

In these periods of life, kids get very easily fixated on objects or activities, so the lure of a new experience or simply a change of scene is usually sufficient to make them forget their initial activity.

Therefore, when you see your child doing something you don't approve, such as crayoning the walls, before explaining to him or her why this is not a good behavior, try and offer an alternative just as appealing, such as a squeaky toy.

The secret here is not to only offer the toy, but for you to start playing with it and make it look like you have so much fun. Kids try to imitate parents, so it is very likely that they would find your activity much more fun than what he or she was doing. Talk to your kid while playing with the toy because your voice alone is sometimes enough to distract a child.

Of course, this procedure can have ups and downs. Sometimes, your child will need a more powerful redirection, and this is why this technique is also called "*changing the scene*".

If you see that your efforts remain without results, talk about the tempting aspects of a different room or going outside. Take the child from its initial spot and offer a more suitable alternative for its activity.

Don't think that this method is bulletproof because it doesn't always work. However, most of the time, redirection lets you avoid punishing or acting in an unwanted way while trying to educate your child.

7. Set clear boundaries and expectations and be consistent.

A very big mistake you can make is to assume that kids don't have the ability to finding loopholes in your boundaries.

This is why setting limits for children is a very challenging task. A lot of mothers and fathers consider that the best way to set boundaries is to use the word "*no*" from the moment of birth until the day the child becomes an adult. This kind of parents also make a huge mistake when talking about limitations. They don't conceive a big set of rules that need to be abided but invent new ones every day only because they seemed to fit at that time.

We already talked about how setting the correct boundaries will help your child to grow life skills, so I won't linger too much on this aspect. I will provide you a simple guideline to help you understand the correct way to establish these limits.

Once again, prevention comes in the discussion. If you think about possible situations and all of the potential issues that can occur, you can save yourself from a lot of trouble later. For example, teach your child there is no cookie before dinner and explain how this is a house rule.

Explain your expectations as much as you can without turning into a nagging parent. Make sure that these expectations are clear and positive. Therefore, focus the discussion on "*do's*" and not on the "*don'ts*".

Another secret that I discovered is that if you want your limits to really be successful is to let your child know the reasons for the imposed limits. So, if you want your kid to pick up his or her Lego toys, don't use sentences such as, "*You better put your toys where they belong when you finish playing.*" Instead, try and say, "*Baby, don't forget to pick up your Lego. You don't want somebody to step on them and destroy them.*"

Break big tasks into smaller parts. This way, you will be able to make them understand and at the same time, you will be able to keep your expectations simpler.

Remember that if you want your rules to be respected, you have to respect them yourself. Kids mimic our gestures, so don't ask your child to act in ways that you can't just because you want to. For example, don't eat pizza in front of your son or daughter if you want them to eat healthily.

Lastly, while we are on the subject, keep in mind that we all make mistakes. Therefore, setbacks and breaking boundaries are normal for every family. Whenever you encounter this kind of situation, just gently remind your child what are the house rules and start over. Of course, don't forget to let him or her face the consequences that come from breaking the rules.

8. Use single word remedies or questions or state facts, instead

of ordering or demanding compliance

Again, children have small attention spans. This means that if you give instructions that are too long, they will lose their interest very soon after you open your mouth. This is especially true when you try to educate your child into doing something they don't want to.

Another possibility is your kid answering back on one of your demands, simply because they feel like there is a chance of not abiding your rules.

However, it is amazing how well the use of just a single word can make your disciplining task easier. Let's understand how this actually works.

So, if you use neutral words, you will help your child to quickly form associations. Therefore, it is more likely he or she to listen to your command. But you should be careful about what words you pick. For example, terms such as "*no*", which we all know we tend to overuse, are not so effective. The reason for this is that even though it is a standalone word, it doesn't actually give any instructions or indications for the child. On the other hand, if you use words like "*pause*" or "*stop*", your kid will know exactly what is demanded.

Imagine you have two children, and one of them is hurting his/her brother while snatching a toy. If you simply say "*no*," the child will not understand what part you refer to. Yet, if you say "*stop*", the infant will know that they have to stop hurting their sibling.

If you are not a person of few words, then you can apply a slightly different approach that is known to give equally good results. Stating facts is known to be just as effective and parents who wish to communicate their demands in a more lengthy way really appreciate it. I won't let you wonder too much about how this works, and I will finish this bullet point with an example that will serve as the explanation.

Let's say that you want your kid not to throw rocks. If you just say *"don't do that,"* most probably, you will not have any kind of success. But if you go on and state the fact *"If you do not stop, you will end up hurting somebody,"* you will definitely see a positive reaction.

9. Work as a team to come up with a mutually-agreeable solution (problem-solving)

It is scientifically proven that kids tend to accept and respect the house rules more if they are part of their creation. This is why positive discipline encourages working together to come up with a mutually-agreeable solution. If you don't know how to approach the discussion or how to invite your child to talk about the boundaries he or she must comply with, let me suggest implementing something that can be called *"family meetings"*.

I want you to think of these gatherings very seriously and prepare for them just as you would prepare for a work meeting. By doing so, you will show commitment to your family. [21]

A great thing that I have learned from these meetings is that they provide an opportunity to discover so many things about your child and therefore to better understand their wants and needs. Furthermore, just as important, it will help your kid to understand you, your demands and expectations as a parent, and also the reasons behind them.

For home staying mothers, this idea might sound crazy. Why on Earth would you need to plan a meeting with your child? Unfortunately, the number of working parents is huge and for this category, setting regular family gatherings will create special moments.

The secret of successful family meetings is respecting each member's opinion, regardless of how futile they might sound. You want to encourage your child to speak freely, and you won't be able to do so if you crush their ideas and cut their wings.

Suppose you are talking about eating healthy meals, little Jack comes and proposes to have a pizza day once a week, don't react by saying, "*This is a ridiculous idea.*" The correct approach would be to suggest to have a regular pizza day once a month and to introduce a healthy cauliflower recipe from time to time.

This is why discussing rules with your child is so effective. You can meet in the middle and find solutions that will please both you and the youngsters. This kind of experience will help your child to develop important skills such as solving problems or learning how to accept the opinions of others.

Try to keep the meetings calm. It won't serve anyone if you get mad and start yelling. However, if it happens to have a contradictory discussion, make it end on a positive note. By doing so, every family member will remember the gathering as a good one and will look forward to the next meeting.

10. Allow the kid to face the consequences (natural consequences, not made-up consequences to suit your needs)

The final bullet point positive discipline is based on is related to the consequences of undesired behavior. What makes this technique different than other disciplining tools is the type of consequences you present to your child.

It is safe to say that consequences can be logical or natural. The logical ones require the intervention of others while the natural ones, well, they come naturally, and these are the ones you should base your education on.

For example, if you want your child to take on another jacket when going outside, don't say, *"Put on a jacket, or you won't go to the school trip!"*. If you use this approach, the kid will most likely take the extra clothing just to make you happy and will wear it only until they are out of your sight. However, if you say "*Darling, you should take an extra jacket with you. It is cold outside and you might get cold and miss the school trip*," the situation will be in your favor.

Even though natural consequences are a very powerful tool when disciplining kids and should be used as your main strategy, there are some cases in which you need to make use of logical ones. For instance, you don't want your child to experience the natural consequence of eating poisonous fruits or going into deep water without knowing how to swim. Also, you don't want for him or her to learn the natural consequences of hurting other people or acting cruelly against animals.

For all the situations above, you will need to learn how to establish logical and easy to understand consequences so your child will keep away from them, but this is a topic for a different chapter.

Positive Parenting

We are down to the last part of this book section. We are talking since the beginning of the text about what positive discipline is and how it should be applied, so naturally, it is time to look in the mirror and see what kind of parenting we use. In order to do that, let's see what positive parenting is.

I am confident that at this point in the book, you know that positive parenting has nothing to do with indulging your child to get away with too much but about providing education without making use of humiliating or scary manners. Yet, what does that actually mean?

Well, it means many things, and I want to start by saying that it is about giving the child the feeling of belonging.

We all need to feel like part of society or a group, and along with this need, there comes the desire to be a significant member of it. So don't assume that children, just because they are young, don't have the same desires and needs.

Of course, you, as a parent, are responsible for providing clothes, food, and a roof over their heads. But how can you make sure you offer the other aspects which are just as important for a healthy growing up? To understand this, we need to talk about the meaning of belonging. So, when you feel being a part of something, you actually feel wanted and since we are social creatures, we long to be part of something bigger than just ourselves.

For a child, the notion of belonging is even more necessary and can be very easily rocked. Just by the birth of a sibling, a child can start feeling less important and left behind. But if you understand where these thoughts originate from, you'll be able to approach them adequately.

By doing so, we can talk about positive parenting. To continue with the same example, a positive parent will make a child who just got a sibling and who feels like they not being number one anymore to know what his or her significance is.

This being said, before a new baby enters your family, be sure to talk to your elder child and explain the changes that will occur in the house and how his or her help is needed to care for the newborn. This way, your child will not only feel needed when the time comes, but they will also feel like part of something greater than themselves.

However, if you make sure that your child knows the feeling of belonging and significance, it doesn't necessarily represent that you are raising him or her in a positive parenting fashion. Other aspects need to be taken into consideration.

Every time the kid misbehaves, you need to remind yourself that his or her action is just the result of a greater problem. So, what positive parenting teaches us is that we don't have to punish the child for misbehaving but to find the root of the issue and eliminate it. Just imagine a water hose that has a hole in it. If you put a patch on it, the water will pour out eventually and the only way to solve the issue is to turn off the water supply until the hose is replaced.

The same applies when trying to correct an undesired behavior of a child.

The mistake that many parents make is to consider misbehaving children to be bad or defiant. This is what positive parenting is trying to correct. It considers every child misbehaving to be a cry for help for an issue that needs grown-up assistance.

But let's see exactly what are the full effects of positive parenting.

First of all, it **maintains a quality relationship between parent and child**. This kind of relationship is the one that sustains the development of a child, regardless if we speak about physical, emotional, or social growth. In my perspective, this kind of bond should exist between every child and its parents. I am sure that nobody can contradict me when I say that this parent-child connection is the foundation of the child's future relationships and personality.

Therefore, positive parenting makes sure that children grow happy and have a healthy family relationship that will lead to social and academic skills and good cognitive abilities.

Every child-parent connection is different, and therefore, there is no exact science of how to build a strong bond. However, some little tricks can consolidate the connection.

For example, play as much as you can with your child, and every now and then, let him or her know how much you love them. Also, let your child know that even if you have a job, you are always there when he or she needs you. Last but not least, listen to your child's problems and empathize, regardless of the subject.

Of course, other means work just as good. The conclusion is to spend as much time with your offspring as possible without spoiling the child and refusing him or her a personal social life.

Another effect of positive parenting is teaching children how to **take responsibility for their actions**. What parent doesn't want to raise a competent child? Unfortunately, not all actually do it successfully.

So all parents want to know how to educate their kids to become accountable for their choices and their influence on society?

Well, the first step is to raise your child letting him or her know that every action has a consequence, and you will not always be there to clean the mess they make.

At every age, your child will need guidance to overcome life challenges and take the blame when he or she makes a mistake. If you teach your child, in a positive way, that every action triggers a reaction, you will notice that regardless of the child's age, you will not receive a too defensive response towards your education.

For example, if your girl, Mary, comes with dirt on her shoes and leaves footprints on the carpet, you can tell her calmly, "*Mary, in this house, we take our shoes off before coming into the living room, or else we clean the carpet ourselves.*"

Children can contribute to the housework just as adults. Of course, this is true in accordance with their age. By giving them small house chores in order to receive the desired award such as ice cream money, you teach your child that they need to take responsibility and that nothing in life comes without hard work.

The most difficult issue here is to figure out the age-appropriate responsibilities and not overwork your child or giving him or her less than they can handle.

To make your job easier, I will take each age

period at a time and give you a few tips and tricks that are known to give the children the sense of responsibility they need to become successful adults.

Toddlers

At this age, they are so young, so some would think children can't be given any responsibility. But this is not true. There are some small aspects that toddlers can take responsibility for.

At this very fragile age, kids can be responsible for choosing the toys to play with, asking for the potty or, the amount of food to eat. Of course, none of these can be done without your help, but they represent the first step to more important tasks.

Preschoolers

As they grow, children actually desire to be given more responsibilities. So, this age period is the perfect one to introduce more. For instance, clothing choices, meal options, in healthy parameters, and of course, who to befriend with.

Again, you, as a parent, have the create and offer your child choices from which he or she can choose from. This way, the child will start feeling responsible for its decisions.

School-age

After reaching the age of 6, the child can start actual house chores such as putting their plate in the sink after eating or wiping the table. Beginning with this part of its life, the child is assigned their first very big responsibility - homework.

You can encourage your child to take an interest in practicing a sport or playing an instrument, but in the end, the decision to take responsibility for such an activity lays in his or her hands.

Preteens

At this age, children start wanting more and

more independence and with it the possibility of earning money to buy games, clothes, or gadgets. Therefore, you can offer more house duties, such as taking out the garbage or washing the dishes. As a reward, they can receive pocket money and can use their allowances.

This is also the perfect age to let your child walk home from school if the road is not dangerous or stay at home by themselves for a few hours with the condition of respecting your rules.

Adolescence

This is the last chance you have to teach what responsibility is, so be sure to use it wisely.

This being said, let your child be responsible for the means of transportation to take when going out or cleaning the house.

The biggest change which this period brings is the possibility of taking a job as a babysitter or other age-appropriate career. By starting a career, they take full responsibility for their actions and their earnings.

Positive parenting **teaches children what is respect and how to be respectful to others.** So instead of talking of the "*why*", I will focus more on the "*how*".

Firstly, kids imitate your reactions, so be sure to treat your child with respect even when they misbehave.

However, there are cases in which even though you treat your child in no disrespect manner, he or she thinks to behave differently towards others. Fear not! Positive parenting encourages us to use their actions to teach them what to do and what actions to stay away from.

As a parent, you are in the position of letting your child know that even adults make mistakes and that it is ok to apologize when such situations occur.

By doing so, your child will not only know how to be respectful but also know how to correct their errors.

I remember my mother saying that in the end, the most important thing you need to teach children is to know the difference between right and wrong. Since it is such an essential topic, I will not delay stating the fact that says positive parenting is exactly what you should use to help your child **knowing what is right and what is wrong**.

We all want what we want, but kids don't usually know the dangers that some desires can bring along. Thus, it is our responsibility to explain to them how the world works and how it is not only a pretty, happy place.

What positive parenting brings, in addition to other parenting methods, is the calm approach that kids find easier to listen to and abide by.

At the end of the day, kids need to learn **how to make decisions on their own**. Therefore, these decisions should be wise.

Being a good parent doesn't mean to make choices for your kid just because you know better. This is why every positive parenting technique suggests you let your child make choices from a very early age, and even more, they recommend to let your child make mistakes of their own only to learn from them.

Lastly, if you will positively educate your kids, you will teach them how to be **honest, loyal, and trustworthy.** All of these qualities are the result of the aspects previously discussed, so instead of wasting your time and repeating the same information, I propose to you a new chapter fully dedicated to misbehaving.

CHAPTER SIX

A NEW LOOK ON MISBEHAVIOR

I told you that I have a full chapter on the subject of misbehaving, but I want to take a look with fresh eyes on the matter. If we take a moment and contemplate this topic, in most of the cases, children are not even doing something wrong and their actions falsely pass as inappropriate acting.

So, once again, if we take a new look at what misbehaving is, you can win lots of pleasant moments with your child and not the other way around. As soon as you understand that, most probably, the way your child is behaving is caused by one of your actions or the lack of one, you will be able to correct your approach and avoid the consequences.

At a closer glance, you'll notice that misbehavior is nothing more than a lack of information or adequate parenting skills.

In many instances, kids are just acting their age without doing anything bad. Unfortunately, many adults fail to realize this aspect and the result is that lots of kids are getting punished without any actual reason. [22]

Why children misbehave, and how can we correct it?

There is no correct answer to this question, especially when their actions are misinterpreted. However, just as adults, kids have needs, and if these needs are not satisfied, they tend to be cranky and do things adults don't approve of, such as screaming or throwing stuff. These reasons are usually linked to hunger, tiredness, or previous similar events in which they were "*bribed*" to stay still.

But this is not the topic that I want to highlight.

I want to focus on the moments in which children actually misbehave and the reason why they do it.

In her book, Amy McCready states that a misbehaving child is really a discouraged child [23].

In this case, the term "*discouraged*" describes the moments in which the child isn't receiving a strong enough sense of belonging and significance.

We are all aware of those moments in which children are angry and cling on us for no reason, or so it seems. However, the reality is that the child who acts like that has plenty of reasons for doing so. In a very primitive way, the infant is trying to communicate that it needs to feel as if he or she belongs in your family, and more so, it is significant for its development.

These are the cases in which most children misbehave simply because they need attention and prefer negative attention than no attention at all.

If this behavior is isolated, then you should not worry too much. But if you see your kid repeating this kind of action, you should be aware that the child most probably thinks that only the negative way of acting will help him or her achieve their primary aims of belonging and significance.

We have previously talked about the necessity of offering the child a sense of belonging and significance, and I don't want to come again and state why these feelings are vital for healthy development. What I am trying to state is that children crave these feelings without even knowing about their existence. They just feel incomplete and their primary instincts tell them to act regardless of the method. They try multiple ways to get our attention and keep doing it until they succeed. So, as I've said, negative attention is better than no attention.

You know those moments when you meet someone on the street and start talking for a while and out of nowhere, your kid starts to act crazy and interrupts everything you say? The child doesn't do it because she is not educated, but because she wants all your attention to herself.

Remember when I gave you an example of a new baby coming into the family? Most elderly siblings struggle to regain their feelings of belonging and significance and act inappropriately. I consider this to be a very delicate matter, one which can not be solved with a handshake on the street when meeting a friend and providing the child your full time. Because of this, I want to move our focus a little to the cases in which the child has siblings.

Even if you don't intend to raise more than one kid, I still suggest you give this part a look. You never know what life has in store for you.

So, it is clear as day that only children receive all the attention in the world from their parents and therefore, they are more likely to know exactly what the feelings of belonging and significance are. Yes, it is true that since they are the sole receiver of their parents' love, they can become spoiled and lose the significance feeling. This directly depends on how the parents interact with the child and can be rectified if it is noticed.

Moving on, let's start the discussion of what happens when the family has more than one child. Firstly, in the case of the firstborn, for a while, he or she will have the same characteristics as only children do, because well, at least for a year they will be only children. A firstborn has the chance to develop strong emotional bonds with their parents and have the opportunity to understand how being the most important person in the room feels like.

However, if a second baby comes into the family, things change, and if you are not careful, your firstborn will show signs of regression instead of progression. Why?

Well, let's take the example of Mary. Mary gets a little brother, Jack. Mary will see that every time Jack cries, he receives attention regardless if it is about wetting a diaper or receiving a cuddling moment. So, in her mind, Mary will not understand that Jack doesn't have the ability to request food or he is not potty-trained. She will see it just like this - Jack cries and he receives attention, so why wouldn't she do the same? Even more, why wouldn't she refuse to use the potty and wet her pants?

This is why the parents need to teach Mary how to be responsible and how to take care of Jack. For example, give Mary the responsibility of watching Jack and see he doesn't lose his pacifier when going out. Or let Mary cuddle him and play with him just as much as you do. By doing so, Mary will not only feel like a family member again but as a very important one, without whom the family cannot survive.

If we move our focus to Jack, we can notice that he has every reason to develop a strong sense of belonging. If Jack would to remain the last member that enters the family, he will be forever the "*baby*" of the house, regardless of his age. Since he is the youngest child, he might have issues in finding his sense of significance, simply because there are so many older family members to take responsibility for him and do his work.

So, your responsibility, as a parent, is to carefully give your youngest child lots of chances to make significant contributions to the family.

The situation for Jack becomes even more complicated if he turns into a middle child and gives the youngest position to little Charlie. By this time, Mary is well aware of her position in the family and how she is your right hand when it comes to house chores, but the situation will not be as easy for Jack.

He will find himself in no meaningful position. He will neither be the firstborn and therefore have a great significance in the family, nor will he be the baby anymore. The truth is that usually, middle children report a weak sense of both belonging and significance.

So, in order not to make your middle child feel lost, be sure you give him, if possible, even more attention than the other two. The best approach is, of course, to distribute your time and their responsibility equally. Unfortunately, we know that this theory is impossible to apply, so the best thing you can do is to distribute them accordingly with their age and necessities.

In short, just remember that you have to induce the same sense of belonging and significance in all your children, regardless of how many they are.

Change in Belief, Not Just the Behavior

Now that you understand the reasons why children really misbehave and understand a thing or two on how to help them overcome difficult moments, I wish to talk about another aspect of correcting children's misbehavior.

Unfortunately, there are not very many adults who are involved in childcare that understand how behind every behavior, there is a belief. Because of this, they don't look for motivation, but they just try to change unwanted behavior. What they don't know is that a misbehaving kid can and will only stop when the belief behind their motives is changed.

The truth is discovering the motivation behind the action your kid does is not very easy. This is why Jane Nelson actually offered a *"Break the Code"* model that is designed to aid you in understanding why your child behaves in a specific way.[16]

You will have to read her book in order to see exactly how she proposes to handle these situations. It is her technique, and rewriting it or making a summary will not do it justice.

However, I will tell you this. Breaking the code

behind your child's misbehavior includes understanding what triggers an undesired action, identifying the child's feelings, and of course, learning how he or she is calmed down.

After realizing the core of your child's problems, you will not only be able to prevent them but you will also be capable of changing the child's beliefs if they are wrongly making him or her misbehave. Or why not, you will be able to change yourself if the child's beliefs are the correct ones.

CHAPTER SEVEN

CONSEQUENCES

Since we had a full chapter on misbehavior, it is natural to have one about consequences to follow it.

As you know, even though for a child, punishment and consequences might look the same, they are actually very different aspects of discipline. This is why, before anything else, I want to address the subject of consequence types.

Logical Consequences vs. Natural Consequences

This being said, there are two major consequence types, which we have already briefly discussed. Therefore, I won't linger too much on making an introduction of these classes. I will say, as a reminder, that I am referring to the natural and logical consequences which can be used as a response to children's actions.

Even though I am more inclined to use natural consequences, I cannot say that I don't see the necessity of the logical ones as well. This is why I strongly believe that parents who use both techniques to teach their children how to behave do a better job than the ones who only apply one type of consequence. However, this is something that you need to decide on your own. It is simply my duty to give you all the information you need in order to make a decision.

Natural Consequences

As their name suggests, natural consequences happen directly as a result of actions, and they don't require any adult involvement. For example, putting a hand on a hot pot will induce pain or pulling the cat's tail will get you scratched.

Usually, children learn fast from natural consequences, especially when pain is involved, such as the hot pot case. In other situations, kids need to repeat the process in order to understand how their actions led to undesired situations.

So, what is the role parents need to play in natural consequences? Well, parents don't have a very important part. They just need to allow them to happen naturally until the moment they are not safe anymore.

I know that it breaks any parent's heart to see how his child suffers as a result of their action. You feel pain when they get stung, you feel hungry when they refuse to eat, and you feel heartbroken when they are dumped. But letting your child live and overcome all these aspects of life will prepare him or her for the moments in which you will not be around to offer your protection anymore.

Sometimes natural consequences are far more painful for the child than lengthy lectures from you. If Mary cuts her hand using a scissor, which you particularly told her to stay away, don't give her the "*I told you so*" speech. She already realized that you were right and she will keep her hand away from that scissor and will most likely listen more to your next pieces of advice.

Unfortunately, there are cases in which even if you don't want to, you will have to take charge and not rely on natural consequences.

First of all, you should not rely on natural consequences when the health of your child is at stake. Another situation would be when the consequences don't come fast as a result of the child's action. If they are delayed, the kid will not make the connection between the two and thus will not learn from their errors.

Logical Consequences

On the opposite side of the natural

consequences when parents just need to watch and let the events take their usual course, the logical ones are imposed by the caregivers. The first thing I want to highlight here is that they are different from punishment, and I will tell you exactly why is this.

Firstly, a logical consequence is not given as an immediate response to your child's action. You have to plan them in advance and not let anger overcome you. By planning and discussing them with your child, the consequences will be relevant and straightforward.

In the ideal situation, you state the consequences before any situation may occur. Yet, we know that this is not always possible, but you can at least state them for a future re-offense.

The most effective method to ensure the success of a house rule is to discuss the logical consequences with your child and create them together as he or she grows up.

Probably the most important part when establishing logical consequences is to make them have a connection with the correlated misbehavior. Therefore, for breaking a curfew, cutting off the TV access doesn't make too much sense. But if you don't permit your child to go to the next party, well that is a consequence that he or she will remember the next time they want to stay late without your permission.

Also, the logical consequences should not only be connected with the child's actions but need to be neither too strong or too weak, and of course, they need to be consistent.

I remember talking to my partner one time when our child broke one of our house rules. It was a minor issue, and I wanted to let it go, and I would have done a very bad thing if I would have listened to my heart. However, I listened to my partner who said: "*Honey, if we let her go with this, she will use it against us for other more serious issues.*"

So, inconsistency is out of the question when it comes to consequences.

Just as natural consequences, logical ones also have some applicability limitations, but if you make some rules in advance, you should not have too many issues.

Three Rs and H of Logical Consequences

Since it is your responsibility as a parent to establish the logical consequences, you need to know the full details of this subject, and the full details include something known as the three Rs and an H, representing related, respectful, reasonable, and helpful.

Related

As I previously said, the consequences you decide for breaking your rules need to be connected to the child's actions.

These need to be in correlation because if not, the child will not understand the cause-effect link.

By providing related consequences, you will be able to focus on individual accountability for the child's actions, and you will not be "*blamed*" for what will probably be perceived as punishment.

Respectful

Respect needs to be present regardless of the situation. Only by setting a good example, your child will learn that in life in order to receive respect, you have to offer it. So, even if your child has broken a rule that brought down a logical consequence, you still need to apply it with respect.

This means that you need to stay calm and try as much as possible not to raise your voice. Speak directly to your child without using names or sarcasm. Be clear, and don't let room for any negotiations.

Reasonable

Of course, any logical consequence needs to be within reasonable limits. Don't expect your child to pay for a misbehavior with something impossible to give. Be sure that you put a normal timeframe for the consequence. If you tell your kid he or she will stay grounded for the rest of their lives, well, they will not take you seriously. Timeframes are different depending on the child's age and should be set accordingly.

Helpful

The logical consequence should be helpful in such a way that your child will learn something from their mistakes, even if you are the game master. So, don't imply that if the child suffers from what he or she considers to be a punishment, you kid will actually learn something from this experience.

Therefore, it is your responsibility to come up with logical consequences that will help your child in the future.

Four Rs of Punishment

The goal of telling you all this is that, if you don't set the consequences using these guidelines, you will most probably find yourself having a child that suffers from one or more symptoms of the four Rs of punishment. These are **resentment**, **revenge**, **rebellion**, and **retreat**.

There isn't much to say about these four aspects that are not logical and straightforward. Therefore, I will just make a short presentation.

Children that feel resentment consider that the consequence they receive is actually an unfair punishment, making not only parents but adults in general not to be trusted.

The revenge feeling also comes from improper consequences and will make your child want to get even as soon as possible. From this emotion, another R is born, and I am talking about rebellion. A rebellious child will not only want to get even with you but will want to act in such a way to ensure you get mad.

The last symptom that can result from inappropriate punishments is retreat. This can mean two things. Either your child will improve their techniques of getting away, therefore keeping many secrets from you or will develop very low self-esteem and think that everything he or she does is bad.

I am sure that if you are a normal and loving parent, you don't want your child to acquire any of the four R's characteristics.

So, the hard truth is that usually, parents only use punishment as a form of demonstrating the power over the child. This being said, if you ever want to use the "*I am the adult, and you are the child*" approach, just think of how you make your child suffer.

As a conclusion, I want to remind you again that logical consequences are not the answer for every wrong action of your child. You should let him or her learn on their own how life responds to actions, of course, within the limits of safety.

Don't invent a logical consequence for every small behavior possibility and therefore restrict every self-discovery for your kid. Instead, use the natural consequences to teach your child about pain, respect, work, and self-esteem.

CHAPTER EIGHT

FOCUSING ON SOLUTIONS

The biggest problem most parents have is that they focus on the wrong aspect when it comes to their children's education. What does that actually mean? It means that instead of focusing on the solution, they focus on the problem, which leads to a negative approach.

It is unfortunate, but very frequently, parents react rashly and before listening to the reason for which the child misbehaved, they go on and forbid whatever is most important to their child. If your child has a special talent or hobby, such as dancing or practicing a sport, it is not wise to take it away from him or her. This activity, since it is very important for the child, if removed, it will affect the child's self-esteem and should not be used as a trade good.

Thus, is so important to focus on the solution

and not on the problem. If you do it successfully, you won't make the mistake of damaging your kid's growth.

But in order to do that, you need to be able to have good communication with your child, and this is exactly what I want to talk about next. Known as positive communication, this approach concentrates on really listening to your kid's needs.

I noticed that generally parents when giving a lecture to their offspring don't actually want to be heard, but they want to be obeyed. That is the most wrongful approach ever. Normally, children will consider this a struggle for power and will defy most of what their parents say.

Another truth that I discovered and of which I already briefly talked about is that kids have a short attention span, so the likelihood of them listening to all you have to say is close to none. Also, if you keep talking without giving your child the chance to speak and for you to listen, why would the kid do it? We already know that kids mimic our gestures. Therefore, if you want him or her to listen to what you have to say, teach him using the power of example.

So, if you want to be a good model for your child, start by asking and not telling. Encourage your kid to talk about his or her feelings and needs.

The first step in doing so is being empathetic with everything your child is going through. Listening and acknowledging their daily problems is the key to positive discipline.

You already know that kids want to be recognized and listened even though at the beginning of their lives, kids don't even know what feelings are tormenting them. In the early years, you can name emotions and explain each one so your kid can understand what they are feeling and tell you.

Listening to and acknowledging children's emotions will not only help them open up to you but will also help them recognize emotions and develop better compassion and prosocial behaviors.

If you want to really understand a child's feelings, you have to open your sole and talk about yours as well.

Therefore, discuss your wants and needs and, while doing so, try to connect even at a physical level. When children feel loved with every atom of their body, they are more likely to cooperate. Remember that connection alone can calm your child down when the emotions are too high.

However, the secret for healthy communication is to accept that your child has thoughts and feelings that he or she needs to share with you. Of course, you don't have to agree with all of them, but you have to listen to what he or she has to say.

Most likely, your ideas and his or her opinions will not match, but if you manage to connect at a profound level, you will be able to brainstorm and find a mutually agreed solution.

Remember that we have talked about family meetings? So, planning a meeting with your child to adjust rules and consequences is the right thing to do. Present him or her a list of debatable and non-debatable aspects and be prepared to discuss it.

Allow your child to carefully look at the list so it can be prepared for the conversation. Don't forget to ask the child if he or she wants to make additions to your list. It is of no use if you are only willing to talk about your points of interest. Listen carefully to everything he or she has to say and don't reject any topics even if they sound ridiculous to you. Remember that you are brainstorming for solutions and not forcing your point of view. In these situations, it is helpful to take notes. If you manage to agree on an aspect, write it down and make your child repeat it. This way you can be sure that he or she truly understands the rule and the consequence it brings if broken.

Don't forget that compromises need to be made by both sides. Of course, you cannot compromise when it comes to safety, but you can compromise on little things such as an extra half an hour for the curfew.

Try and agree to as many points as possible which your child proposes, but be prepared to also disagree. Over-reacting will produce more damage, so try to keep your calm as much as possible even if you hear ideas that you find to be absurd.

Lastly, not every problem has an easy solution, and therefore, it cannot be done with a simple brainstorm. If a satisfying bargain cannot be reached on a particular matter, set it aside for a few days and let it rest. There are many cases in which a solution isn't clear until a day or two later.

Positive discipline concentrates on encouragement and not on praise. So, rather than glorifying children for a job done well, you should better concentrate on your child's struggles even if the result isn't successful.

Encouragement and support from your side will help kids understand their full potential. It also prepares them to become independent while growing up.

Every little thing you do regarding your child will influence their life. Because of this, it is safe to say that your personality will affect your kid's character.

It is also safe to say that personality has an impact on almost every area of a person's life. This includes relationships, careers, and quality of life. From a psychological point of view, we can say that you, as a parent, have the power to influence your child's five leading personality traits. These features are known as the "*Big Five*" and are agreeableness, openness, extraversion, conscientiousness, and neuroticism.

A study done by Amaranta D. de Haan, Maja

Dekovic, and Peter Prinzie of Utrecht University researched how the parents' personalities and the ones of their adolescents can affect the parenting dynamic. [24]

They speculated that friendly and social parents would most likely present assertive and very motivating behaviors with their sons and daughters. On the opposed pole, introverted mothers and fathers would behave in a more reserved and unavailable manner.

The researchers discovered that children with complex and difficult characters or children who are careless and distractible may receive a severer discipline along with negative feedback from their parents.

The team studied especially the kindness and over-reactive discipline. I can say that the results are more than fascinating.

They found that over-reactivity was affected more by the parent's temperament rather than the adolescent's character. Although the same cannot be said about warmth. This is affected by both children's and parents' character traits.

As you can see, the way you treat your child will affect its full life from the moment you give birth to him or her to the moment of their death.

CHAPTER NINE

SUPPORT

We are down to the last chapter, and I must confess that there aren't many facts that you haven't heard so far. This is why I have dedicated this final part to support and therefore to some last tips and tricks.

Positive Discipline at Home

Firstly, I want to focus on household education, which is not only the first one your child receives, but it is just as important as the one he or she gets at school.

To be able to apply good positive discipline at home, the first thing you need to do is to control your own emotions and learn how to be calm and patient. In other words, you need to understand feelings better so you can teach your child how to manage its own feels.

You will require this knowledge if you want the advantage when the time comes and you need to establish the bond between you and your child. You will want to build the strongest possible connection with your kid because infants who feel connected to their parents usually want to please them and they feel this as second nature and not as a requirement.

Of course, even with a strong child-parent bond, kids will misbehave, so what you need to do first is to reaffirm this connection and never, not even for a second, let your child feel disconnected from you.

Every house has its rules, and your offspring should also abide by them. Therefore, don't delay the moment and set boundaries as soon as possible, but be sure to do it with empathy and with your son's or daughter's help. Understand their perspective and make compromises. When kids feel that they are heard, they're more likely to accept the imposed limitations.

Even if it is hard to believe resistance and rebellion are not age characteristics, but they indicate relationship issues between you two. There is no better clue to make you realize that what happens with your child is strictly linked to the education you give. Don't worry! You are not the only parent who makes mistakes in this direction. The secret is to recognize your errors and correct them in terms of strengthening the relationship.

Whatever you do, don't ever hit or humiliate your child. If you do so, you will not only traumatize your infant but will also show that this kind of behavior is ok and therefore, the child can use it in its relationship to others.

Yes, kids imitate us, so don't tell them to follow rules that you can't. Teach your child that for every action, there is a reaction and let him or her learn the natural consequences of their behavior when safety allows it. Don't spoil your child by doing everything on his or her behalf. This will just send him or her unprepared into adulthood.

Positive Discipline in the Classroom

For a child to grow up and turn into a healthy adult, it is not enough to receive a positive discipline at home, but they need to get the same treatment at school as well.

Actually, positive discipline is a more efficient way to handle and guide misbehaving students in the classroom, rather than applying punishment or rewards. This is true because this technique enables students to discover and adjust their behaviors to meet teachers' expectations and, at the same time, learning how to make better choices on their road to adulthood.

So, when a student is misbehaving in the classroom, teachers must have a few methods that they can apply to discourage or eliminate undesired behavior. If a teacher uses a positive discipline approach, both the pupil and supervisor will be able to understand what is the cause of the problem and what are the expected consequences for misbehavior.

Of course, these consequences need to apply for every possible occasion and should be applied with calm. Just as parents, the very important aspect teachers need to understand is that there is a difference between punishment and consequences, differences I will not explain again.

However, I will say that the impact of punishment on students can be very damaging. This includes causing physical or emotional discomfort and even not being efficient in decreasing future misbehaviors.

On the other hand, positive discipline is the practice of education that will ensure the students obey the needed behavior system. Therefore, rather than controlling the behavior of students, scholars can apply positive discipline to develop a child's actions through self-control.

Each teacher can choose what positive behavior approach to take as it seems fit. From setting up rules at the beginning of the school year to listening when students have something to say, educators are their own masters. Yet, in the end, everything reduces to one aspect - love.

Love and Joy in Homes and Classrooms

It is not enough to receive love only at home, but it is just as important to feel it in the classroom. You might ask yourself why, and I think that discussing the need for love at home is redundant, and I should not waste your time with that. Instead, I will focus on why it is important for children to feel love also when they are at school.

Well, mostly, because love motivates children.

Even us, as adults, we don't want to stay in places where we are not valued and cherished, and you don't have to be a mastermind to realize that students feel the same.

If children feel that they are loved when they are in the classroom, they are capable of opening themselves up and experience a very beautiful feeling known as joy. Unfortunately, nowadays, humankind has forgotten how to be happy and how to handle joy. But if you help children find this kind of emotion and even more to find it when studying, you will allow students to realize their highest potential.

We all know that in order to succeed, we need to make mistakes from which we can learn. Therefore, students need to feel safe and should not be scared to make mistakes, regardless if we are talking about the incapacity of solving a math issue or talking disrespectfully to a teacher.

Unfortunately, very few teachers understand

that in order to help a child overcome these problems, the best weapon is love.

If a teacher infuses a classroom community with love, a multitude of impacts can be noticed. Even though this proof is sometimes small, it is still important. So, don't have enormous expectations. Remember that every gesture counts, and love cannot be measured.

This being said, without being ready to make a connection between teaching, learning, and love, we cannot expect to meet the best results for students. Therefore, we cannot continue to talk about subjects such as success or results without turning our focus to the learning circumstances in which students either thrive or flounder. The universal truth and I am happy to finish the book with this word, is love.

CONCLUSION

First of all, I want to congratulate you. I imagine that staying there and listening to someone instructing you on how to educate your child is not an easy thing to do. You are a better person than me, I must confess. So, since you did manage to finish, what I hope was a helpful and easy-to-read book, I want to make a small recap of what we've discussed.

After all this information lectured, you know what positive discipline is, how it works, and of course, the benefits that this kind of education brings along.

We have discussed what are the techniques necessary to approach children based on their age period and how to act when children misbehave. We have explained how and why sometimes adults misinterpret how kids act and therefore consider them to be misbehaving.

Another very important factor we have gone

through was the presentation of the differences between natural and logical consequences and when to use each of them.

As you can see, all the information from this book was shortened in a few lines, so it is nothing too complex. This means that every parent can and should adopt this disciplining model. In the end, these are all just fancy words and procedures for what is actually the best way to educate a child

I can write another book in this part, but you probably don't want to read any more on this subject. You now have the information to understand positive discipline, so the best thing you can do now is to start implementing small changes in your child's education. After this, finish the day in any way you want, but please go to bed with the conviction that tomorrow is the first move you take in providing your kids with the best education possible.

The most unfortunate thing you can do now is to delay the process. So let's start the correct

Daniel Faber

disciplining of your child!

REFERENCES

[1] Rudolf Dreikurs and Vicki Soltz, (1964). Children: The Challenge

[2] "Madison Metropolitan School District Student Conduct and Discipline Plan" (PDF). Retrieved 14 January 2016.

[3] Center on the Developing Child. (2009). Five numbers to remember about early childhood development

[4] Raby, K. L., Roisman, G. I., Fraley, R. C., & Simpson, J. A. (2015). The enduring predictive significance of early maternal sensitivity: Social and academic competence through age 32 years, Child Development, 86(3), 695–708.

[5] Cassidy, J., & Shaver, P. R. (2016). The handbook of attachment: Theory, research, and clinical applications (3rd ed.). New York, NY: Guilford.

[6] Ten Bensel RW, Rheinberger MM, Radbill

SX. (1997) Children in a world of violence: the roots of child maltreatment. In: Helfer ME, Kempe RS, Krugman RD, eds. The battered child. Chicago, IL, University of Chicago Press

[7] Kempe CH et al. (1962) The battered child syndrome. Journal of the American Medical Association, 181:17–24.

[8] Straus MA et al. (1998). Identification of child maltreatment with the Parent–Child Conflict Tactics Scales: development and psychometric data for a national sample of American parents. Child Abuse & Neglect, 22:249–270.

[9] Youssef RM, Attia MS, Kamel MI. (1998). Children experiencing violence: parental use of corporal punishment. Child Abuse & Neglect, 22:959–973

[10] Hahm H, Guterman N. (2001). The emerging problem of physical child abuse in South Korea. Child Maltreatment, 6:169–179.

[11] C. M. Charles, Emeritus, San Diego State University, Gail W. Senter, California State University San Marcos, Karen Blaine Barr, California Public Schools, (1999). Building Classroom Discipline, 6th Edition

[12] Berger KS (2003). The Developing Person Through Childhood and Adolescence (6th ed.). Worth Publishers.

[13] Antisocial behavior. Encyclopedia.com. Archived from the original on 25 March 2018.

[14] de Terte, Ian; Stephens, Christine (2014). "Psychological Resilience of Workers in High-Risk Occupations". Stress and Health.

[15] Sukhodolsky DG, Smith SD, Mccauley SA, Ibrahim K, Piasecka JB. (2016). Behavioral Interventions for Anger, Irritability, and Aggression in Children and Adolescents. J Child Adolesc Psychopharmacol.

[16] Nelsen, Jane (2006). Positive Discipline.

[17] Bell SM, Ainsworth MD (1972) Infant crying and maternal responsiveness. Child Dev

[18] Kohlberg L. Development of moral character and moral ideology. In: Hoffman ML, Hoffman LW, eds.(1964) Review of Child Development Research. New York, NY: Russell-Sage Foundation

[19] Janet Lansbury. (2014). NO BAD KIDS: Toddler Discipline Without Shame

[20] Jane Nelsen, Ed.D., Cheryl Erwin, M.A., Roslyn Ann Duffy, (1994). Positive Discipline for Preschoolers: For Their Early Years

[21] Jane Nelsen, Ed.D., Cheryl Erwin, M.A., Carol Delzer, (1994). Positive Discipline for Single Parents

[22] Jane Nelsen, Ed.D. (2011). The Classic Guide to Helping Children Develop Self-Discipline, Responsibility, Cooperation, and Problem-Solving Skills

[23] Amy McCready (2011). If I Have to Tell You One More Time...: The Revolutionary Program That Gets Your Kids To Listen Without Nagging, Reminding, or Yelling

[24] Haan, A. D., Deković, M., & Prinzie, P. (2011). Longitudinal Impact of Parental and Adolescent Personality on Parenting. Journal of Personality and Social Psychology.